20 FUN FACTS ABOUT BULLFROGS

BY THERESE M. SHEA

Gareth Stevens
PUBLISHING

Please visit our website, www.garethstevens.com. For a free color catalog of all our high-quality books, call toll free 1-800-542-2595 or fax 1-877-542-2596.

Library of Congress Cataloging-in-Publication Data

Names: Shea, Therese, author.
Title: 20 fun facts about bullfrogs / Therese M. Shea.
Other titles: Twenty fun facts about bullfrogs
Description: New York : Gareth Stevens Publishing, [2021] | Series: Fun
   fact file : North American animals | Includes index.
Identifiers: LCCN 2019047822 | ISBN 9781538257586 (library binding) | ISBN
   9781538257562 (paperback) | ISBN 9781538257579 (6 pack) | ISBN 9781538257593
   (ebook)
Subjects: LCSH: Bullfrog–Juvenile literature.
Classification: LCC QL668.E27 S54 2021 | DDC 597.8/92–dc23
LC record available at https://lccn.loc.gov/2019047822

First Edition

Published in 2021 by
Gareth Stevens Publishing
111 East 14th Street, Suite 349
New York, NY 10003

Copyright © 2021 Gareth Stevens Publishing

Designer: Sarah Liddell
Editor: Kate Mikoley

Photo credits: Cover, p. 1 (main) LorraineHudgins/Shutterstock.com; file folder used throughout David Smart/
Shutterstock.com; binder clip used throughout luckyraccoon/Shutterstock.com; wood grain background used
throughout ARENA Creative/Shutterstock.com; p. 5 Ilias Strachinis/Shutterstock.com; p. 6 Steve Bower/
Shutterstock.com; pp. 7, 10 (female) Michael Benard/Shutterstock.com; p. 8 Elizabeth W. Kearley/Moment/Getty
Images; p. 9 sonomafoto/iStock/Getty Images Plus/Getty Images; p. 10 (male) Sue Bishop/Shutterstock.com;
p. 11 Michael G McKinne/Shutterstock.com; p. 12 Ivan Kuzmin/Shutterstock.com; p. 13 Ty Hartlipp/Shutterstock.com;
p. 14 Isabel Eve/Shutterstock.com; p. 15 Mircea Costina/Shutterstock.com; p. 16 sasapanchenko/iStock/Getty
Images Plus/Getty Images; p. 17 Jerry Regis/Shutterstock.com; p. 18 Alexander Boehm/EyeEm/EyeEm Premium/
Getty Images; pp. 19, 23 (egg) feathercollector/Shutterstock.com; p. 20 Suwatwongkham/iStock/Getty Images
Plus/Getty Images; pp. 21, 23 (froglet) Karakirky/Shutterstock.com; p. 22 Yves Forestier/Contributor/Sygma/Getty
Images; p. 23 (adult) Ute Sonja Medley/Shutterstock.com; p. 23 (tadpole) Suwat wongkham/Shutterstock.com;
p. 24 wasin suriyawan/Shutterstock.com; p. 25 Tom Grundy/Shutterstock.com; p. 26 Jim Beers/Shutterstock.com;
p. 29 Dwayne Towles/Shutterstock.com.

Printed in the United States of America

Some of the images in this book illustrate individuals who are models. The depictions do not imply actual
situations or events.

CPSIA compliance information: Batch #CS20GS: For further information contact Gareth Stevens, New York, New York at 1-800-542-2595.

Find us on

CONTENTS

Words in the glossary appear in **bold** type the first time they are used in the text.

BIG BULLFROGS

Several species, or kinds, of frogs are called bullfrogs. All are large for frogs! This book is about the amazing bullfrog of North America. Its **adaptations** have made it a successful animal in different **habitats** around the world. Some of these adaptations are odd. Others are gross. All are interesting!

Read on to learn more about this **amphibian**, known as the American bullfrog. This frog species has spread all around North America. Bullfrogs might live near you!

Scientists sometimes call the American bullfrog by its scientific name: *Lithobates catesbeianus.*

LARGE FROG, LARGE MOUTH!

THE BULLFROG IS THE LARGEST NORTH AMERICAN FROG.

Bullfrogs weigh about 1 pound (0.5 kg). That's a bit more than a football weighs! They can grow to be 8 inches (20 cm) long, with their legs tucked under them. Their back legs are even longer!

A bullfrog's back legs can be 10 inches (25 cm) long!

6

Male bullfrogs may call out to tell other bullfrogs to stay out of their territory.

THE BULLFROG IS NAMED FOR A LOUD NOISE IT MAKES.

Some think the noise that male bullfrogs make sounds like a bull's moo. It's low and loud. People say the call sounds a bit like: "jug-o-rum, jug-o-rum."

This bullfrog has swallowed the tail of a water snake!

FUN FACT: 3

BULLFROGS EAT ANYTHING THEY CAN FIT IN THEIR MOUTHS.

And these frogs have large mouths! They eat bugs, spiders, mice, fish, fish eggs, birds, worms, frogs, snakes, turtles, bats, and many other animals. Bullfrogs even eat other bullfrogs!

BULLFROGS HAVE STICKY TONGUES!

A bullfrog may use its front legs like arms to stuff large prey into its mouth!

Like all frogs, bullfrogs have really fast, really sticky tongues. They use their tongue to seize prey, or the animals they eat, and bring them into their mouth faster than you can blink! The tongue is so sticky because of the frog's special spit.

THE BULLFROG BODY

YOU CAN TELL IF A BULLFROG IS MALE OR FEMALE BY ITS EARS!

Frog ears are called tympanums. They're found on the sides of the head near the eyes. A male's tympanums are larger than his eyes. Females' tympanums are about the same size as their eyes or smaller.

MALE

FEMALE

A bullfrog's tympanum looks much different than a human's ear—it is a large, round area near the eye.

This bullfrog is warming up in some morning sunlight.

A BULLFROG'S BODY TEMPERATURE GOES UP AND DOWN WITH THE TEMPERATURES AROUND IT!

Amphibians are cold-blooded animals. Their bodies need warmth in order to operate well. That's why amphibians, including bullfrogs, are more active when the weather is warm.

FUN FACT: 7

BULLFROGS HAVE SPREAD REALLY FAR FROM THEIR NATIVE HABITAT.

They're native to North America east of the Rocky Mountains. Now, they're as far west as California and Mexico. They've also made it to parts of South America, Europe, and Asia.

12

People brought some bullfrogs to new places on purpose because frog legs are used as food. Some bullfrogs were carried to other places by mistake though.

Bullfrogs spend most of their time in water. They can be seen at the water's edge too.

BULLFROGS HAVE MANY KINDS OF HOMES—BUT ALL ARE NEAR FRESH WATER.

Bullfrogs don't live in salt water. They can live in lakes, rivers, ponds, **marshes**, and anywhere fresh water is mostly still. They prefer warm water that's not too deep.

Polluted water also helps bullfrogs hide from predators.

FUN FACT: 9

WATER POLLUTION CAN BE A HELP TO BULLFROGS!

Waters that have been polluted by people tend to be warmer and have more plants. These features are bad for many animals. However, they make a good habitat for bullfrogs to grow and reproduce, or produce young.

BULLFROG BEHAVIOR

MALE BULLFROGS WRESTLE!

The green frog is another kind of frog that wrestles. These two may look like they're hugging, but they're actually wrestling over territory!

Male bullfrogs prefer to live alone in their territory. To get other male bullfrogs to leave, they sometimes fight. A bullfrog's territory can be from about 10 to 82 feet (3 to 25 m) along the water's edge.

15

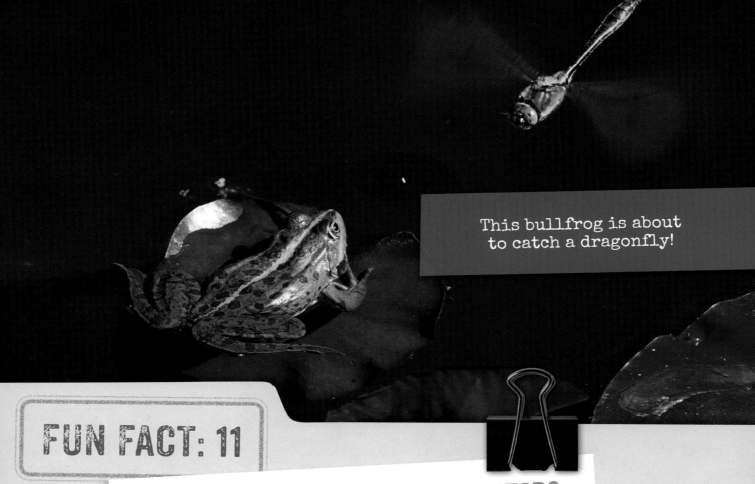

This bullfrog is about to catch a dragonfly!

FUN FACT: 11

BULLFROGS ARE AMBUSH PREDATORS.

This means they don't hunt for prey actively. Instead, they sit still and wait for prey to come near them. When something tasty appears, they leap toward it with their back legs and seize it.

BULLFROGS HIBERNATE.

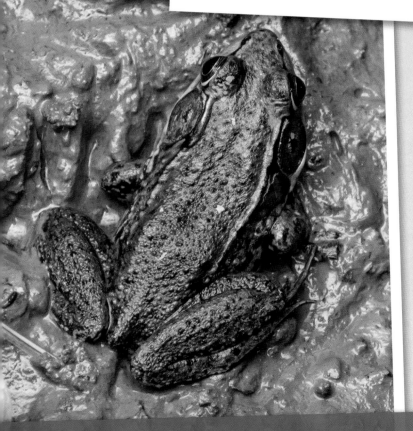

In places where it doesn't get cold, bullfrogs don't hibernate.

Bullfrogs prefer warm weather. When the weather turns cold, some dig into the mud and hibernate, or go into a sleeplike state, through the winter. Some build a small area like a cave. Bullfrogs breathe through their skin while hibernating!

17

A frozen hibernating frog might look dead—but it's not!

A HIBERNATING BULLFROG CAN PARTLY FREEZE — AND STILL LIVE!

Parts of the frog's body can freeze. Its heart may stop, and it may stop breathing too. But some of its body doesn't freeze. When the frog **thaws**, it seems to come back to life!

18

GROWING UP BULLFROG

FEMALE BULLFROGS LAY AS MANY AS 20,000 EGGS AT A TIME!

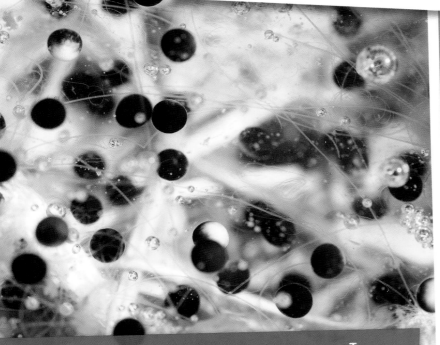

Bullfrogs lay eggs once a year. In the North, this may happen from May to July. In the South, it may happen from February to October.

They lay them in a calm part of the water. A male bullfrog then **fertilizes** the eggs. About four days later, bullfrog tadpoles hatch, or come out of the eggs.

Bullfrog tadpoles are spotted.

FUN FACT: 15

BULLFROG BABIES TAKE CARE OF THEMSELVES!

A bullfrog tadpole comes out of its egg with **gills** and a tail.

It doesn't look like a frog yet. Its parents aren't around to help it.

It eats bugs, **algae**, and plants it finds in the water.

BULLFROG TADPOLES HAVE POISON ON THEIR SKIN!

As bullfrog tadpoles get larger, they grow legs and lose their tail. They become froglets, or young frogs.

You might think fish would eat bullfrog tadpoles. Luckily for bullfrog tadpoles, they taste bad to most fish because of a poison on their skin. Adult bullfrogs have poison on their skin too.

21

THE LARGEST TADPOLE EVER FOUND WAS 10 INCHES (25 CM) LONG!

This bullfrog tadpole, found in Arizona, was wider than a can of soda! Most bullfrog tadpoles take up to three years to grow into an adult. This one never became an adult.

Bullfrogs become adults that can reproduce when they're 3 to 5 years old.

THE BULLFROG LIFE CYCLE

EGG

TADPOLE

FROGLET

ADULT

A life cycle is a set of stages through which a living thing goes, from its beginning to its death. Bullfrogs in the wild can live up to around 10 years.

HARMFUL AND HELPFUL

BULLFROGS MAKE A LOT OF TROUBLE!

They eat so much that other animals go hungry. Females lay many eggs, so bullfrogs spread quickly too. There often aren't enough predators in non-native habitats to keep bullfrog numbers down.

Bullfrogs can hop miles to find another body of water to live in.

The frog species called the mountain yellow-legged frog is in danger of dying out. The deadly chytrid fungus some bullfrogs carry could kill them off.

BULLFROGS MAY BE SPREADING A DEADLY FUNGUS.

Some scientists think bullfrogs have been carrying and spreading a fungus that is killing some other kinds of amphibians. As bullfrogs have moved across the United States, they could be spreading illness to other creatures.

MANY ANIMALS—INCLUDING PEOPLE—NEED BULLFROGS FOR FOOD!

Animals that eat bullfrogs include turtles, water snakes, raccoons, and large water birds such as herons and kingfishers. Some people eat frog legs too. Some states have a frog-hunting season!

This blue heron has just caught a large bullfrog.

26

HOW BULLFROGS HELP AND HARM

HELP

- EAT BUGS THAT ARE PESTS TO PEOPLE

- ARE STUDIED BY SCIENTISTS TO LEARN MORE ABOUT ANIMAL BODIES

- ARE A SOURCE OF FOOD FOR PEOPLE AND ANIMALS

HARM

- CAUSE OTHER ANIMALS TO DIE OUT IN NON-NATIVE HABITATS

- MAY SPREAD A DEADLY FUNGUS TO OTHER AMPHIBIANS

- SOMETIMES GET INTO AREAS MEANT TO RAISE FISH FOR PEOPLE TO EAT, HARMING THE SUPPLY

Bullfrogs are helpful to people in some ways. They're more harmful in non-native habitats where they have fewer predators to keep their numbers down.

THE FUTURE OF BULLFROGS?

People continue to try to keep down bullfrog numbers in different ways. Many of these **solutions** can have bad effects on their habitats. Poisons meant to kill bullfrogs can kill plants and other animals. Introducing non-native bullfrog predators can be harmful to other animals and plants too. Sometimes drying up ponds works, but bullfrogs can just hop away to the next place!

Keep learning about this frog species. Perhaps someday you'll be the scientist who finally solves the American bullfrog problem!

Next time you hear a deep, low "moo" near a body of water, see if you can spot an American bullfrog!

GLOSSARY

adaptation: a change in a type of animal that makes it better able to live in its surroundings

algae: plantlike living things that are mostly found in water

ambush: a surprise attack

amphibian: an animal that spends time on land but must have babies and grow into an adult in water

fertilize: to add male cells to a female's eggs to make babies

fungus: a living thing that is somewhat like a plant, but doesn't make its own food, have leaves, or have a green color. Fungi include molds and mushrooms.

gill: the body part that aquatic, or water-dwelling, animals such as fish use to breathe in water

habitat: the natural place where an animal or plant lives

marsh: an area of soft, wet land that has more grasses than other types of plants

solution: something done or used to solve a problem

thaw: to melt

wrestle: to fight by gripping, holding, and pushing rather than hitting

FOR MORE INFORMATION

BOOKS

Albertson, Al. *American Bullfrogs*. Minneapolis, MN: Bellwether Media, Inc., 2020.

Harrison, David L. *And the Bullfrogs Sing: A Life Cycle Begins*. New York, NY: Holiday House, 2019.

Hesper, Sam. *Bullfrogs*. New York, NY: PowerKids Press, 2015.

WEBSITES

American Bullfrog

kids.nationalgeographic.com/animals/amphibians/american-bullfrog/
See beautiful bullfrog photos and learn more about these creatures here.

American Bullfrog

www.biokids.umich.edu/critters/Lithobates_catesbeianus/
Check out this great source for bullfrog facts.

INDEX